**This book is a "must read" if y[ou ...]**
**15 questions on this leadership [...]**

1.___Are you regularly visible and avai[lable ...]

2.___Do you take time to train staff on a [re]g[ul]ar basis?

3.___Do you regularly delegate tasks that help your staff to grow and also free-up more of your time?

4.___Do you empower staff members when giving them responsibilities and make that empowerment known to others?

5.___Do you exhibit a "turn lemons into lemonade" attitude and set the example to help motivate staff to meet challenges?

6.___Do you regularly turn staff mistakes into positive learning experiences?

7.___Are you respectful of your subordinates' time?

8.___When you call for a meeting do you set a written agenda and time limit and stick with it?

9.___Do you keep staff regularly informed to avoid rumors spreading?

10.__Do you regularly recognize others for their accomplishments, no matter how small?

11.__Do you allow your staff to do certain things differently from you as long as the task is accomplished properly or do you micro-manage to have things done the way you would do them?

12.__Do you regularly review responsibilities and workloads to be sure they are fair and balanced throughout your staff organization?

13.__Do you give undivided time to subordinates rather than work on unrelated things simultaneously when they meet with you?

14.__Upon returning from being away for a while do you thank the people on your staff for "minding the store" in your absence?

15.__Do you regularly share the vision, mission and goals of your department and the company so that your staff knows what they are working towards such as: posting quarterly financial goals and earnings as well as weekly stock closing price and other significant financial information?

**RLD Institute**

"*If I had eight hours to chop down a tree, I'd spend six hours sharpening my ax.*"

- Abraham Lincoln -

# Dedicated to...

**Mary Ann,** my wife who has always awed me with her ability to lead a husband and four children, always making us feel that we were the center of her universe.

**Lennie, Beth, Mike** and **Ann,** my children who, as they arrived into this world, made me fully realize the meaning of accountability and responsibility.

**Those whom I've served with in the United States Marine Corps,** from generals to the newest recruit, all believed that the leadership that the Corps offers is the finest of any organization in the world.

See last page for how to order additional copies of this book

Printed in the United States of America
Third Printing 2013

ISBN 0-9725091-9-4 (Volume I)
ISBN 978-0-9725091-9-0 (Volume I)


Published by

**RLD Institute**
P.O. Box 2557
Gilbert, AZ 85299
602-573-0745
www.ThoughtsWhileShaving.com

## *Forward*

The reason for this book is to offer leaders, and followers, simple yet profound ideas that go right to the heart of leadership: *Integrity, Character, Loyalty, Passion*. *Real Leaders* continually prepare followers to be leaders and provide the means in the organization for everyone to grow and excel.

While growing up, I found that I always had two different types of teachers. One type would be the *Intimidator,* "Just do what I say, sit down, and be quiet!" **The other type would lead by suggesting, offering appropriate rewards, and punishments, always looking to bring out the best in the individual.** The latter always seemed to have a following made up of former students who always appeared comfortable being in their presence.

Leaders that I have followed over the past fifty years have either been *Intimidators* (one of my bosses, I hesitate to call him a leader, once told me, "I only give compliments if you're dead or I'm dead drunk!") or *Real Leaders*, someone encouraging me to perform at my best. *Real Leaders* create a bond through their leadership style that lasts a lifetime. I consider the *Real Leaders* in my life good friends and mentors.

The *Real Leaders* in my life were great simplifiers. They all believed in the *KISS* principle (Keep It Simple Stupid). They were leaders in large complex organizations, yet everyone from the janitor to the board of directors knew what the organization was all about and where it was going.

*Real Leaders* have made a significant difference in my life. It is my goal that through this book, the principles of *Real Leaders* will make a difference in your life.

*Len Fuchs*

**1** If you are leading a boring meeting, in a boring conference room, you can't expect much beyond boring ideas.

**2** If your change effort isn't working - change it.

**3** Leaders should beware of off-sites that create a momentary adrenaline rush, but do nothing to facilitate change. Successful off-sites link great (or new) ideas to real world issues.

**4** Any change effort that requires more than one page to articulate its goals is doomed to failure. If the point of the change is complex, people lose focus - and eventually lose their way.

**5** Too many times, people (and organizations) wrongly emphasize activity rather than performance.

**6** Focus relentlessly on the things that move you toward your goals, but as you close in on the goals never lose sight of the big picture.

*Managers are people who do things right; Leaders are people who do the right thing.*

Warren Bennis author of *LEADERS*

**7** Being innovative is when you act on an idea.

**8** Ideas can come from anywhere at anytime. The problem with making mental notes when you have that great idea is that the ink fades very rapidly - write it down.

**9** When the leadership shows that they truly pay attention to ideas, even the small, seemingly insignificant ones, then an environment is created in which people feel comfortable generating and offering productive ideas. People feel valued and respected and the creative energy will be felt throughout the entire organization.

**10** The ability to state the problem is often more effective than the solution.

# These were written the week after...
## 9/11

**11** Americans are leaders.

**12** Americans are world leaders.

**13** American leaders support justice and condemn evil.

**14** American leaders must make decisions that are very difficult, but do what is right, because it is the correct thing to do.

**15** Americans will follow leaders who have integrity and dignity.

**16** American leaders ask for God's blessing upon America and the world.

**17** People are more creative when they are on the edge and required to think out of their comfort zone.

**18** Leadership skills are better than rules. Leadership skills assist you in determining what is right and what is wrong.

**19** One way to achieve goals and accomplish tasks quickly is avoid "reinventing the wheel."

*Experts should be*

*on tap, not on top.*

Winston Churchill

**20** Providing personal growth opportunities is the greatest reward for a motivated individual and it pays great dividends back to the organization.

**21** If you never hear laughter in your organization, you're doing something wrong.

**22** Many times you never have enough time to get everything perfect, as the leader you must decide when enough is enough and make the decision.

**23** Effective leaders define the right goals and then let the individual find his own route in achieving those goals. Decisions made at the lowest possible level allow things to get done more efficiently.

**24** Ideas energize an organization.

**25** Organizations that are well established have to go beyond business as usual by creating new initiatives to challenge their people.

**26** An organization will never figure out where it is going if it doesn't take a cold, hard look at where it is coming from. Be brutally honest about where your organization is.

*People have a way of living up to*

*your expectations.*

Anonymous

**27** Leaders should have a personal exit strategy. You are not going to want to run a company/organization forever. Step aside when the mission (or market) has to change, otherwise you are going to run the company/organization into the ground.

**28** Passion is created by new challenges.

**29** If you want to build or strengthen an organization the most important question to ask is, "What needs are we serving?"

**30** Leaders know that people are looking for the opportunity to do something worthwhile.

**31** Good leadership is like water, air, food - people crave it and good leadership is not rejected.

**32** The better you know people in your organization, the better you can lead that organization.

**33** With so much information available the only way to learn is to keep changing.

*You can't escape the responsibility of tomorrow by evading it today.*

Abraham Lincoln

**34** Reward people for achieving specific goals and producing results that fulfill the organization's mission. Reward people for the right behavior, and you'll get the right results; rewarding negative behavior steals the motivation of achievers and attracts people who are mediocre.

**35** As a leader if you are not informed, it shows.

**36** Leaders create a sense of purpose, excitement, and fulfillment in an organization.

**37** Successful organizations take advantage of the expertise of their partners, suppliers, distributors, resellers, customers, and most importantly, their employees.

**38** Leading is a relationship, not a transaction.

**39** Good leaders offer values, humility, straight talk, and a genuine point of view.

**40** Leaders must sometimes deliberately create chaos in order to affect change. Chaos forces everyone in an organization to ask, "Who are we? What do we stand for? What are we doing?"

*A great leader never sets himself above his followers except in carrying responsibilities.*

Jules Ormont

**41** Our own fear of the unknown, and of failing professionally, sometimes prevents us from pushing our employees to be more flexible.

**42** If you fail to articulate the real mission of your organization you deny what gives meaning to the members of the organization.

**43** Leaders can affect how we think, what we decide and ultimately what we create.

**44** Today the organization chart is becoming hyper-linked, not hierarchical. Respect for hands-on knowledge many times wins over respect for abstract authority.

**45** Leaders know that people want more choices and are prepared to shoulder the consequences of those choices.

**46** The job of a leader is to help people make the right choices.

**47** Effective leaders force people to the limit of their abilities, to do more than what is comfortable.

**48** Leaders help people visualize success. It is easier to understand success by talking about behaviors than by talking about revenues.

*The higher in rank you go, the more people look to you to set examples.*

Maxwell D. Taylor

*People follow a leader, not because they have faith in him, but because he has faith in them.*

Anonymous

**49** Leaders help members of their organization answer the question, "How is change relevant to what I do?" If employees can't answer that question on their own then the grapevine will provide the answer - and that answer is usually wrong.

**50** Successful leaders have the ability to see things as they are, not as they wish they would be.

**51** As a leader one of your biggest competitors is your own view of the future.

**52** Leaders move organizations patiently and persistently, because inertia doesn't give way quickly.

**53** Culture is one of the most elusive terms in an organization; you change a culture by changing the behavior of the people.

**54** Becoming a leader is a marathon, not a sprint.

**55** There is nothing more dangerous than a leader with a closed mind.

**56** Every one in the organization becomes more productive when their leaders work smarter and respect people's time.

*Greatness does not depend on the size of your command, but on the way you exercise it.* Marshal Foch

**57** Leaders usually get things done executing their current strategy rather than continually debating a new one and accomplishing nothing.

**58** Leaders create value in their organization through the power of their ideas and the authenticity of their character.

**59** Success is what brings an organization together, not parties, special gatherings, bonuses, etc.

**60** Leaders get the behavior they allow.

**61** Good employees help their leaders lead.

**62** Part of the art of leadership is picking out the organizational segments that are willing to try something new.

**63** Leaders create value in their organization through the power of their ideas and the authenticity of their character.

**64** Leaders have the skill and ability to dig deep when the need arises to get past the short-term pain and do what is best for the organization in the long run.

**65** People who are busy pointing fingers and whining about "those guys" (or that department) are demonstrating their lack of leadership.

**66** Effective leaders attract a crowd of good people around them.

**67** Leaders often find that forward motion is as important as which route to take.

**68** Leaders listen to the whole idea before starting to develop an even better solution.

**69** Leaders don't stop until they are finished and when they do stop they are preparing to start again.

**70** One way thinking can lead to a dead end.

**71** Leaders believe in the power of first hand knowledge.

*You cannot be a leader and ask other people to follow you, unless you know how to follow too.*

Sam Rayburn

**72** Individuals who lead by coercion usually focus the organization against them.

**73** If you can never speak from personal experience, you are not going to convince many people.

**74** Leaders must have a "teachable point of view," that defines what they want the organization to achieve and how the organization will do it. This "teachable point of view" must be conveyed in a form that others can readily learn and teach in turn.

**75** As a leader you are provided with many signs, but you have to be willing to see those signs.

**76** If you want to communicate with people about change, you first have to change yourself.

**77** Leaders are aware that large companies have great camaraderie and, as a result, they can be insulated from a lot of what is really happening in the organization.

*One of the tests of leadership is the ability to recognize a problem before it becomes an emergency.*

Arnold H. Glascow

**78** Leaders don't try to do what in their hearts they know they can't.

**79** Leaders understand that things don't always work out. The faster you pinpoint a problem, the more quickly it can be solved.

**80** The fuel that drives leaders must be substantial; something for the heart that the mind can follow.

**81** When the other guy is on your turf, you have to do what is unexpected.

**82** Leaders have the ability to edit out the noise that comes disguised as information.

**83** Leaders bring a willingness to learn.

**84** Leaders make sure their message is consistent.

**85** Leaders don't have to be fast, but they must remember that they are running a race that has no finish line.

**86** No matter how careful you are as a leader, some risk can't be avoided.

**87** Leaders hear what they need to know and inspire what they need to do.

**88** Leaders understand that knowledge is only useful if you do something with it.

**89** In order to lead, you have to command people's attention - and steal their hearts.

**90** Leaders don't make excuses.

**91** Leaders don't work for themselves; they work for everyone, the entire organization.

**92** The best grounding in leadership comes from knowing who you are.

**93** Effective leaders strengthen others.

*One of the best leadership abilities you can have is the ability to recognize ability.*

Anonymous

**94** Many believe that leaders should exhibit depth and profundity at all times. But, in fact, the goal should be learning, changing, and playing.

**95** Leaders understand that without passion it is just a job and organizations without a soul are just a shell.

**96** A leader is trusted.

**97** Because of the increased pace in business and life in today's society there seems to be little time for reflection. Reflection allows leaders to build on both experience and intelligence.

**98** Leaders transform organizations and the people in them.

**99** Leaders make emotional connections.

**100** People are always hungry for work that is exciting and meaningful.

**101** Effective leaders have the ability to zero in on a multitude of operational details, without losing sight of the big picture.

**102** In order to sustain change everyone needs to be part of that change. People don't respond well to the "Lone Ranger" coming in to save the organization.

**103** Successful organizations have people at all levels who will take risks and make decisions.

**104** There are organizations that have off-sites at exotic locales, make lots of big plans, then go back to work and do nothing about the great ideas. That organization's leadership philosophy: There is no good idea that can't be stifled.

**105** Leaders avoid individuals who are experts on everything except how to get things done.

**106** The leading organizations of the future will be the ones whose leaders can react easily and quickly to the world around them.

**107** Leaders don't get tied up in endless strategy meetings looking for the perfect solution.

*Never tell people how to do things.*
*Tell them what to do and they will*
*surprise you with their ingenuity.*

George S. Patton

**108** There is nothing wrong with leaders possessing power. The wrong comes when power possess leaders.

**109** If you don't have "Smoke Jumpers" in your organization, then the leadership will be putting out fires instead of leading.

**110** Leadership is not about having the answers; it is about being open enough to keep asking questions.

**111** Effective leaders have initiatives that connect with employees. These initiatives make employees want to perform and stay with the organization.

**112** Most leaders don't realize how unique they are, how powerful their role is, or how hard their task.

**113** Some leaders see something unusual and assume that it is wrong. However, leaders who are innovators have the ability to see something unusual and recognize that an answer may lie in its difference.

*A man who enjoys responsibility*
*usually gets it. A man who merely*
*likes exercising authority usually*
*loses it.*

Malcolm S. Forbes

**114** Leaders who want to carry an idea forward, designate a battle captain who is clearly responsible for that idea and is authorized to make it happen.

**115** Leaders recognize that what makes individuals different also makes then creative.

**116** Leaders understand that innovation doesn't have to be complex and that everyone has the ability to make innovation happen.

**117** Standards help make creativity possible by allowing for the establishment of an infrastructure which then leads to creativity and competitiveness.

**118** The greatest enemy of creativity in an organization is fear.

**119** Leadership is a higher form of selling. What you are selling is the future.

**120** Companies/organizations routinely underestimate what it takes to execute a new idea.

**121** Effective leaders can step back, see what is really needed, and acknowledge when they don't have the resources necessary to achieve success.

**122** Unfortunately some leaders believe that it is more important and more valuable to be clever than it is to have the ability to make something happen.

**123** Constant change is healthier than stability.

**124** Good ideas come when people with different perspectives work together on the same problem.

**125** One of the most important communication skills a leader develops is being a good listener, rather than making everyone else a listener.

**126** If you are waiting for someone else to lead you to a better way of doing business, then it will probably be a long wait.

**127** You will not meet your goals, hit your numbers or make your deadlines - your people will.

*Correction does much, but encouragement does more. Encouragement after censure is as the sun after a shower.*

Goethe

**128** Successful leaders have the ability to discern the important issues and keep the real goal in view.

**129** Many leaders don't realize that reaching the summit is optional, getting back down is not.

**130** Successful organizations continually look at where they stand and what they stand for.

**131** Leaders must allow for contradictions, uncertainty, and ambiguity and they must allow new things to emerge - even when those things are unexpected or unpleasant.

**132** Leaders must be able to communicate risky, potentially revolutionary ideas and at the same time forge broad alliances.

**133** Leaders can pursue their organization's vision with unbridled enthusiasm when that vision is understood and can be clearly articulated by everyone in the organization.

**134** An organization's leader has to be the soul of the company - the living, breathing believer in the company's vision/mission.

*A leader is best when people barely know that he exists. When his work is finished, his aim fulfilled, they will say, "We did it ourselves."*

Lao-tzu

**135** Reaching a mediocre goal is less meaningful than setting a difficult goal and not reaching it.

**136** In an unpredictable world, organizations that treat their employees as people with ideas, rather than interchangeable parts, know how to listen and don't punish experimentation - will win.

**137** Change is hard because we overestimate the value of what we have and underestimate the value of what may be gained by the change.

**138** Leaders understand that an idea doesn't become an innovation until it is widely adopted and incorporated into people's daily lives.

**139** Leaders in an organization are easily recognized by their depth of commitment and the authenticity of their character.

**140** Leaders should challenge their employees to challenge them.

**141** During times of stress leaders should look at it as an opportunity to do something different, either in their leadership style or in the development of those in their organization.

**142** Many times leaders who always wait for approval are waiting for someone to cover their rear in case they fail.

**143** Leaders don't find humility very exciting, but in a humble state their capacity to observe and learn is increased.

**144** Organizations that spend all their time studying things instead of making a decision are hiding from something they are afraid of - the fear of making a mistake.

*Dante once said that the hottest places in hell are reserved for those who in a period of moral crisis maintain their neutrality.*

John F. Kennedy

**145** Successful leaders learn how to ask good questions.

**146** An essential of being a good leader is being a good teacher.

**147** Effective leaders know when to let go; they don't want the organization to become totally dependent upon them.

**148** Leaders should not use sarcasm - it creates the fear that the leader is going to embarrass the employees.

**149** Successful leaders see themselves as guides.

**150** It is difficult to lead unless people believe that you care about them.

**151** A crisis in an organization allows a leader to discover new opportunities.

**152** It costs money to train; training is an investment, not a cost.

**153** As a leader do not judge too early, it is easy picking glamour over reality.

**154** Leaders know that perfection is a mask some hide behind. Sometimes the best answer that gains the most trust is, "I don't know."

**155** Adversity usually takes leaders to something new and often times better.

**156** Successful leaders don't necessarily excel in raw brain power. They tend to question accepted views and to consider contradictory ones.

**157** As a leader you can't change more in your organization unless your people know more.

**158** Leaders don't just listen to their employees; they understand them - personally and emotionally, as well as rationally.

*The higher men climb the longer their working day...There are no office hours for leaders.*

Cardinal Gibbons

**159** Listening is an activity that leaders cannot delegate.

**160** As a leader, it takes courage to select the option that cannot be quantified (to go with your gut feeling).

**161** Politics in an organization can kill any good idea.

**162** A leader's sense of style and powers of persuasion can change an organization.

**163** Leaders challenge the status quo in order to make a positive difference.

**164** The ability to apply knowledge to new situations is a characteristic of successful leaders.

**165** Leaders understand that creativity rewards those who exercise it.

**166** Diversity defines the health of an organization and its leaders.

**167** If a leader loses faith in an organization, the passion of the organization disappears as well.

**168** Effective leaders provide guidance in terms of ideas and values, while the details are taken care of by those who must complete the task.

**169** Ideas that initially appear to get in the way often lead you to someplace new and better.

**170** Leaders know that success is not random.

**171** Leaders who are able to manage the future, predict it.

**172** Leaders are influential, even when they are not the number one person in the organization.

**173** Organizations can never invest enough in their people/leaders if they want them to excel.

**174** Leaders who are good listeners have a competitive advantage.

*Optimism is the faith that leads to achievement. Nothing can be done without hope and confidence.*

Helen Keller

**175** When leaders are on time for meetings it is a sign of accountability and respect for their colleagues.

**176** Some leaders are so concerned with doing that they never spend time thinking.

**177** Leaders and organizations that continually stay energized excel.

**178** An organizations strategy will not succeed if it can't be clearly articulated by the leadership.

**179** Being a leader requires doing things that others can only imagine.

**180** Many leaders see their life as an epic journey where each day is a new adventure.

**181** Don't expect people to always be thankful for everything you do, many times they are not. Leaders should always provide leadership, no matter what the environment.

*Ethics must begin at the top of an organization. It is a leadership issue, and the Chief Executive must set the example.*

Edward L. Hennessey, Jr.

**182** Crises are the experiences from which leaders learn the most.

**183** People who live with a problem can usually solve it better than someone who rides in from headquarters on a white horse

**184** Demonstrating belief in the organization's vision/mission is one of the best motivators a leader can provide.

**185** Leaders recognize that developing products or doing things quickly is a lot like running a relay: Speed becomes meaningless when a handoff from one team is unusable to the receiving team.

**186** The most successful organizations have the clearest vision of where they are going.

**187** The best way to stay "charged-up" as a leader is to do what's been nagging at you.

**188** Leaders may occasionally get battered and bruised, but they never let themselves be defeated.

**189** A leader should be a catalyst, catalysts don't hang around; in other words don't micro-manage.

**190** For a leader it should never be just another day at the office.

**191** Leaders recognize that untapped potential in an organization exists where they least expect it.

**192** Fear of mistakes in an organization retards the flow of information and causes individuals to focus only on the short term and on their own survival.

**193** Why is it that, at the end of many books and seminars, leaders report being enlightened and wiser, but not much happens in their organization?

**194** Innovation begins when rules that don't make sense are questioned.

**195** To have a competitive edge, you need a creative edge.

## *He that is over-cautious will accomplish little.*

Frederich von Schiller

**196** The most successful individuals in an organization are those who know how to be different.

**197** When you educate your customers (and employees) you turn strangers into friends and friends into lifetime customers (and employees).

**198** More and more the traditional organization chart describes a world that no longer exists.

**199** There is no better way to waste time in life than to dwell on the past.

**200** Successful leaders provide an environment in which individuals can make the right decisions regardless of personalities.

**201** Leaders have the ability to endure when there is no success in sight.

**202** Beware of leaders who know everything about their industry or organization; everything is usually about yesterday.

**203** Knowing it *ain't* the same as doing it.

*There is no security on this earth;*
*there is only opportunity.*

General Douglas MacArthur

**204** When too many are involved in making a decision, decisions will take longer to make until there is complete gridlock.

**205** Successful leaders, and organizations, stimulate change and improvement before it is imposed.

**206** Having to choose between two rights helps define the character of a leader.

**207** In order to build a successful organization, leaders first build the people.

**208** Successful leaders are good teachers and successful leaders teach to learn.

**209** Leaders don't try to change people; instead they work to improve them.

**210** Many organizations have potential that is untapped because people stay buried in their jobs.

*Even if you're on the right track,*
*you'll get run over if you just sit there.*

Will Rogers

**211** Leaders, who are clear about the organization's mission, give individuals the freedom to change.

**212** A leader defines an organization's vision and inspires others to achieve it.

**213** Leaders understand that no matter how many facts and figures they have, they can't predict the future, but they can be very well prepared.

**214** Leaders who cut ethical corners will find their final destination disappointing.

**215** When crises are encountered, leaders should ask how the organization can benefit and learn from the situation.

**216** Leaders understand that hope is not a plan or a course of action.

**217** Effective leaders don't confuse "want to do" with "able to do."

**218** The purpose of a leader is to win, not explain defeat.

**219** Leaders who show people respect get respect in return.

**220** Successful organizations need the insight of a leader who is grounded in reality, has the creativity of a dreamer and is inspired by wild-eyed imagination.

**221** Implementation is the real source of competitive advantage.

**222** Even the best idea is only as valuable as your ability to execute it.

**223** Companies don't listen - people do. If you believe that listening to customers (or employees) is one of leadership's critical jobs, then good listening becomes a critical skill.

**224** Leaders understand that things rarely become orderly on their own.

**225** Leaders who embrace change can mold it in a way that benefits the organization.

**226** Leaders have to keep their promises if they want an organization that people trust.

**227** Believing that you can be the best and sacrificing to be the best will motivate followers.

**228** Leaders know that there is nothing that can beat the magic of the human spirit.

> *This is the day which the Lord has made. Let us rejoice and be glad in it.*
>
> Psalm 118:24

**Len Fuchs**, author, speaker, co-founder of Real Leaders Institute, has been there, done that and earned the credentials to offer leadership principles that work. His accomplishments include:

z Founder of executive leadership training company

z Senior vice president of The Government Division of Franklin Covey, Co.

z Colonel, United States Marine Corps (Ret) with over 3,000 hours of flight time

z Squadron commanding officer

z U.S. Government "Drug Czar" in South America

z Program manager in the Global Positioning Satellite System

Len Fuchs (L), during air control liaison duty in Vietnam, with S. Korean counterpart showing that leadership is an international language.

Len adds, *"This all started several years ago when I began offering five to six brief leadership principles once a week under the title of "Thoughts While Shaving." I work on these throughout the week and then every Sunday evening e-mail them to a growing list of subscribers. This book is a result of encouragement to consolidate these leadership principles into a convenient reference format. This has further led to co-founding Real Leaders Institute as a platform to bring principled leadership to organizations world-wide through publications and presentations."*

For information on **LEADERSHIP PRESENTATIONS** for your organization contact us at **RLD Institute** either of these ways:

**Phone: 602-573-0745**

**Website: www.ThoughtsWhileShaving.com**

**Mail:    RLD Institute**
**P.O. Box 2557**
**Gilbert, AZ 85299**

**Thoughts While Shaving,** Common Sense Leadership Principles, Volume I

# Order Form

| Quantity | 1-99 | 100-999 | 1,000-4,999 | 5,000+ |
|---|---|---|---|---|
| Price each | $8.95 | $7.95 | $6.95 | $5.95 |

Copies _____

Book Total $_____

*Shipping & Handling +$_____
(Continental U.S. - $4.00 + 7% of "Book Total" above)

Subtotal $_____

Sales Tax (8.8%- Arizona Only) +$_____

TOTAL $_____

*Orders shipped ground delivery to be received in 7 - 10 business days
For next business day and second business day delivery call: 602-573-0745

NAME_____ TITLE_____

ORGANIZATION_____

PHONE_____ FAX_____ EMAIL_____
(required to process order)
SHIPPING ADDRESS_____

BILLING ADDRESS_____

CITY_____ STATE_____ ZIP_____

PLEASE INVOICE (ORDERS OVER $200), PO NUMBER_____

CHARGE YOUR ORDER:   VISA     MASTERCARD     AMERICAN EXPRESS

CREDIT CARD NUMBER_____ EXP. DATE_____

SIGNATURE_____

CHECK ENCLOSED (PAYABLE TO: *RLD Institute*)

| **Mail** | **Web** | **Phone** |
|---|---|---|
| **P.O. Box 2557** | www.ThoughtsWhileShaving.com | **602-573-0745** |
| **Gilbert, AZ 85299** | | |

Prices effective September 1, 2010, are subject to change without notice. Orders payable in U.S. funds only.
Orders outside of the continental U.S. must be paid by credit card or check drawn on a U.S. bank.
Orders under $200 must be prepaid by credit card, check or money order.

THANK YOU FOR YOUR ORDER

CPSIA information can be obtained
at www.ICGtesting.com
Printed in the USA
LVHW02s0056050718
582672LV00029B/791/P